LIFE SKILLS

COOL THAT ANGER!

Louise Spilsbury

Heinemann Library
Chicago, Illinois

When anger is a problem

How do you deal with your anger? When feelings of anger build up inside, the tension can simply be too much. Some people release this tension in ways that do not cause any real problems, but others release their anger in outbursts that can be bad for them and for other people.

Uncontrolled anger can lead to destructive and sometimes violent behavior. It makes some people shout and become abusive. It makes others throw things or lash out at people. This kind of behavior damages relationships and can leave the people who do it feeling embarrassed and humiliated. And if someone's uncontrolled anger leads them to physically hurt other people or cause criminal damage, it can get them into serious trouble with the law.

Simply walking away from an explosive situation can give a person time to cool off and calm down.

DID YOU KNOW?

In October 2007, in another of a long line of similar school shootings, a teenager in Ohio shot and injured five people before turning the gun on himself. He was angry because teachers had suspended him from school for getting into a fight. If you are unable to control your anger, you risk ruining someone else's life and your own.

Anger management

Anger management helps people control their anger, rather than letting their anger control them. People may not be able to control what goes on around them, but they can control their responses.

Anger management helps people to understand what makes them angry, why they get angry, and when they get angry. Then people are better able to deal with their feelings calmly and coolly. This allows them to defuse their anger and tension before it gets to a point where they can explode.

IS YOUR ANGER A PROBLEM?

Answer "yes" or "no" to the following questions:

1) Do you often get angry?

2) Do everyday and tiny problems make you furious?

3) Is your anger intense enough that you lose your temper and say or do things you regret afterward?

4) Does your anger last too long?

5) Do you find it hard to let go of your anger, so that you are still stewing about an event days after it happened?

6) Does your anger lead to aggression? Does it make you lash out at people, either using abusive words or physical violence?

See page 50 to find out what your answers say about your anger!

Teenage Anger

Teenagers have a lot to cope with: **puberty,** tests and schoolwork, clashes with parents, and other issues such as broken relationships. Many teenagers experience mood swings and anger. This chapter looks at some of the causes of teenage anger and how best to keep calm and cool in those situations.

FACTORS AT PLAY

Both external and internal events can **trigger** anger. Sometimes a specific individual does something that makes a person angry. For example, an opponent may commit a foul on a basketball court. Sometimes it is a particular event that sets a person off, such as if a party someone has been looking forward to is suddenly canceled. Other times anger comes from within, caused by worrying or brooding about personal problems or relationships.

Growing pains

Hormones cause the changes that come with puberty. These chemical messengers travel around the body, giving instructions to the body to change. Physical changes at this time include a growth spurt, growth of pubic, armpit, and leg hair, and changing body shape.

Changes are not just physical, though. Hormones can cause mood swings, and teenagers experiencing puberty may feel confused, upset, or angry. Puberty can also cause emotional changes and mood swings. When a girl's periods start, she may also have to cope with **pre-menstrual syndrome**, which can trigger mood swings and physical symptoms such as headaches, feeling bloated, backache, and stomach pain. On the upside, puberty does not last forever. These feelings are normal, and others have them, too.

Taking control

There is no doubt that puberty can be tough. There will be occasions when your emotions run away with you, but you cannot always use this as an excuse. Your hormones may play a part in your anger, but it also helps to stop and think about what else may be causing you frustration. Everyone has mood swings—whatever their age. Taking time to figure out what it is that is really upsetting you can help you take control, rather than letting it control you.

DID YOU KNOW?

An **allergy** is when a person's body reacts to a substance that does not normally cause a reaction. For example, someone with a milk allergy might get an upset stomach from drinking a milkshake. Food allergies can also cause recurring feelings of anger, but most people are unaware that certain foods could be a problem for them. Have you noticed you get grumpier after eating or drinking certain foods? If so, ask your doctor to do some simple tests to find out if you have an allergy.

If you are feeling upset or moody, it can really help to talk about how you are feeling with a friend, parent, or even a teacher.

THE STRESS FACTOR

Stress is the feeling of being under pressure, whether it be from schoolwork, sports competitions, issues with friends, or frustrations when things do not go as well as you hoped. Stress can be a positive thing because it gives us the **motivation** to get things done, but stress makes some people upset or angry.

Getting it Right

If someone bullies, threatens, or hurts you, the right thing to do is to talk to someone about it. Asking for help is right and is not snitching. If you let it go, the bullying may continue, and if it builds up until it makes you angry, you will find that fighting back only lands you into more trouble. Never fall into the trap of becoming an angry bully, too.

TIP

When you feel yourself getting stressed and angry, it can help to breathe deeply. Breathe in through your nose in long, slow breaths. Hold in the breath for about five seconds. This draws air deep into your lungs and gives your heart rate a chance to slow down. Breathe out slowly. Keep breathing deeply until you feel yourself calming down.

If pressures at school are building up, take some time to figure out what the real problem is and try to get help dealing with it. If you are simply getting behind with homework or a report, maybe you can make a big push to clear it off your desk. If you feel like you are getting behind in class, talk it through with someone, either your parents or a teacher, and maybe get some extra help.

Try to look into the future and think if the thing that makes you so angry now will bother you then. For example, will it still make you angry that you got a B instead of an A on a math test a month from now?

*Victims of bullying, like Tom Cruise, say that bullies can make you feel upset, depressed, and angry. Bullies try to play with or control your emotions. Faced with bullies, the best thing to do is walk away if you can—especially if their **abuse** might trigger your anger.*

Bullies and bullying

Bullying and gangs are often a **flashpoint** for uncontrolled anger or violence in schools. Bullying is when someone deliberately threatens or makes another person feel miserable. Bullying can involve pushing, hitting, or damaging someone's property, as well as name-calling or spreading rumors, threats, or insults. It can even involve ignoring someone or leaving him or her out.

DID YOU KNOW?

Many famous people were bullied when they were young, including *Mission Impossible* movie actor Tom Cruise. He was given a hard time because he had dyslexia, and he changed schools a lot. He still remembers the stress bullies can cause: "So many times the big bully comes up, pushes me," he recalled. "Your heart's pounding, you sweat, and you feel like you're going to vomit. . . . I don't like bullies."

PARENT PROBLEMS

Part of being a teenager is developing your own identity that is separate from that of your family. This can cause frustration and confusion among all family members, and can lead to angry clashes between you and your parents about all sorts of things: your friends, the places you go, and even the clothes you wear.

When you were a child, your parents pretty much controlled everything you did. As you grow older, you start to make more decisions and choices for yourself. This can be hard for parents to accept, and they may try to lay down too many restrictions. It may make you feel as if they do not trust or respect you. It may make you angry that they stop you from doing what you want or do not see your point of view. Some teenagers also get angry because they feel that their parents embarrass them.

Compromise

There are some hard and fast rules that are non-negotiable to parents, such as "no all-night parties." As for other rules, you may be able to reach a **compromise**. For example, say your parents wanted you to continue with extra math tutoring, while you wanted to give up and play soccer with your friends.

Here are some ways you can disagree with your parents without getting too angry or making them angry.

- Try not to put them down. Instead of saying, "That is a dumb reason for not letting me go out," explain why you disagree with their reasons.

- Listen to their point of view. If you listen to them they will listen to you, and you are more likely to have a conversation than an angry argument.

- Avoid screaming. Try to keep discussions on target and do not slip into personal abuse or let a heated argument develop.

Instead of angry arguments, perhaps you could strike a deal whereby you do both—you could continue the tutoring, but cut back the total number of sessions so that you can fit in some soccer as well.

Talk about it

Communication is the key to any relationship. If you offer information about what you are doing, when and where you are going, and with whom, your parents will feel as though they can trust you. They will start to see you as a young adult capable of making sensible choices. If you say too little, it may seem to them that you are being secretive and trying to hide what you are doing.

It can be tough dealing with your parents, but don't walk away from your problems. Try to stick with it and talk things through. They will probably respect you for it.

TIP

Sometimes it helps to write about what is making you angry or frustrated. It can be easier to express things calmly in words. This also gives you a chance to read it through before you give it to your parents to read.

RELATIONSHIPS AND LOSS

Underlying feelings of anger are often linked to relationship issues, such as the divorce of parents, a breakup, a falling-out with a friend, or even the death of someone close. People can also feel a great sense of loss when a friend moves away. Feelings of grief and loss can easily lead to or intensify anger. This underlying anger can fester and then explode when something minor happens.

Many people face problems at school or in their free time when they feel left out, overlooked, or ignored by friends or classmates. It can leave people feeling angry—for example, if their friends go to a party without telling them, or if they feel people are lying about them or to them. It can be humiliating to be put down in public or ignored in favor of someone else. Rejection and humiliation can leave people feeling very angry for a long time.

When love hurts

It can be exciting and romantic to fall in love, but it can also cause problems. Jealousy can make people angry. No relationship will last if one partner is angry and jealous all the time. These people need to talk things over with someone who can help them handle their feelings and deal with their frustrations.

Anger may result when a relationship ends, too. If one partner wants the relationship to continue and another wants to end it, it can be very upsetting for the people involved.

"When we used to argue, my boyfriend said really nasty, hurtful things to me. He said they were just words and he expected me to forget them afterward, but I couldn't. I used to feel miserable and attacked all the time, so I broke up with him."

Leah, 14

Abuse

In some cases teenagers may be struggling with feelings of anger because of past abuse, such as sexual abuse or violence. This is very serious, and that person really needs to talk to a **counselor** who is trained to help him or her work through the trauma. Holding on to past anger can deeply affect life in the present, and it is important to be able to move on.

Here are some ways to help you deal with a broken heart without giving in to anger:

- Share your feelings with someone you trust. Letting your feelings out and having a good cry can be a helpful release.

- Think positively. Sometimes people feel angry with themselves after a breakup, as though they are at fault, but at times like this it is best to focus on your good points and think of the things you have to offer.

- Do something to cheer up, such as watching a movie or going to a concert.

- Try something new, such as joining a club or taking up a new hobby. This is a great way to meet people and make friends.

Taking on a new, fun challenge means you will be busy concentrating on something else. It is a great way to take your mind off your problems.

THE RESULTS OF RAGE

Anger is natural and normal, but keeping it on the inside can cause problems. To start, unexpressed anger can make people bitter, but in the long term these people may start to withdraw from life. Keeping anger in can lead to a loss of **self-esteem** and even to **depression**.

EXPRESSING ANGER

Expressing your anger badly can be as problematic as keeping it in. You could end up harming yourself or others.

Keeping it in

Sometimes keeping quiet about something that made you angry is okay, as angry feelings may fade away. However, when people **suppress** angry feelings, they risk turning that anger inward, on themselves. People sometimes bottle up feelings of anger because they have been raised to believe that expressing anger is a bad thing. Many people grow up in households where families are proud that they never say an angry word to one another. This is not always a good thing.

You may hear toddlers being scolded for being angry, as if being angry itself is an unacceptable, rather than a normal, response.

When anger is unexpressed, people may make nasty comments behind each other's backs, sulk, get quiet, or ignore each other for days.

Getting it Right

- Set realistic goals. If you hope to get a high grade in a subject you struggle with, you may end up angry with yourself for no reason.

- Focus on the positives. Some things, like your height, you cannot change. Focus on the good things, like the fact you are a fast runner or have great hair.

- Try new things and be proud of what you achieve.

"Holding on to anger is like grasping a hot coal with the intent of throwing it at someone else; you are the one who gets burned."

Buddha, founder of Buddhism

Depression

Depression does not just mean someone is in a bad mood or is feeling fed up. Depression is a serious condition that affects every aspect of a person's life. For many teenagers, depression does not show itself in sadness, but rather in suppressed anger. A depressed teenager may feel grumpy, hostile, easily frustrated, or prone to angry outbursts almost

People often say they are depressed if they have had an argument with friends or had a really bad week. Feeling low is miserable, but it only becomes what doctors classify as depression if you feel low for weeks on end and cannot see a way out of it. If you feel like this, maybe you should consider getting some professional help.

all the time. If you think depression may be the cause of your anger, talk to someone—a parent, teacher, or trusted adult friend—about it, take care of yourself, and start addressing the things that bother you.

Self-mutilation

Self-mutilation, or self-harming, is often used as a way to get relief from intense emotions such as anger or rejection. Self-mutilation usually involves people cutting themselves on their wrists, arms, legs, or stomach with a razor or knife, or burning themselves with lighters or matches.

When people find no other way to express their feelings, they may turn to self-mutilation, but the relief does not last, and people who do this risk permanent injury. When people harm themselves, it is serious and they need to get help, tell someone, and figure out other ways to release tension.

Sick from anger

Some people who suppress anger may become sick. A buildup of tension can cause a rise in blood pressure or stomach problems. Uncontrolled long-term problems with anger can also affect your immune system—the body's system that helps to protect it against colds and flu and helps it to recover quickly from viruses and operations.

Anger can also lead people to all kinds of **compulsions**, such as eating disorders or using alcohol or drugs to numb angry feelings. These things invariably make things much worse instead of making them better.

For many people who self-mutilate, the issue is control. They feel they cannot control what is happening around them, but they can control what they do to themselves.

Some people use alcohol as an excuse for angry or violent behavior. However, most adults can have a drink without becoming abusive. Alcohol may simply intensify anger and lead people to risk injury by getting into fights they would normally avoid.

Taking it out on others

Anger is easier to spot in people who let it out or express it in aggressive, or possibly violent, ways. In addition to the immediate negative effects, venting anger using hasty words or actions does not make the anger easier to manage. In fact, releasing anger in the wrong way often increases the intensity of the feeling. This kind of aggression can cause irreversible damage to people, relationships, and property.

Some people have uncontrolled screaming sessions when they are angry. They get red in the face, shout, and stamp. Their anger seems totally out of control and flies out in all directions. This can leave the person feeling ashamed and embarrassed afterward.

Getting it Wrong

Alcohol and anger do not mix. Besides being illegal until you are 21, drinking alcohol can seriously damage your health. If you have a tendency to express anger through verbal or physical outbursts, drinking alcohol will make matters worse by increasing the intensity of those outbursts. Drinking alcohol can lead to violent behavior. In fact, alcohol is involved in half of all violent crimes.

Acts of violence

When some people lose control of their anger, they insult and abuse others, use threatening language or gestures, or get physically violent. They may lash out at the person they are angry with or at others unrelated to their anger. People sometimes commit acts of **vandalism**—breaking things, throwing things, drawing graffiti, or doing other kinds of damage—in an attempt to get rid of their anger. Acting out your anger like this can only lead to trouble, possibly with the law.

Uncontrolled rage can make people do foolish and even violent things. Acting out like this does not solve anything and only puts you at risk of hurting yourself or others.

HOW WELL DO YOU REACT?

1) **You get angry when a friend forgets to invite you to a party. How do you deal with it?**
   a) Explain to your friend why you are upset.
   b) Physically attack your friend for making you angry.
   c) Bottle it up inside and tell no one.

2) **You get really annoyed when you see your younger sister wearing your favorite hat. What do you do?**
   a) Count to 10, then approach her and tell her to ask you before she borrows your things.
   b) Run home and throw all her belongings out of the window.
   c) Let her wear it and don't say anything.

3) **When you get angry, how do you feel?**
   a) Like you have a surge of energy rushing through your body.
   b) Like throwing a punch at someone.
   c) Sad and depressed.

4) **You want to have some friends over for an end-of-the-school-year sleepover. That same night your parents are having a dinner party and so say "no." What do you do?**
   a) Talk to your parents and negotiate to have a sleepover on another night.
   b) Freak out and leave the house, promising never to return.
   c) Feel sick to your stomach.

5) **You've been out on two dates with a person you really like. The person dumps you. How do you deal with the rejection?**
   a) Go and see a movie with a friend and try to think positively.
   b) Throw stones at the home of the person who dumped you.
   c) Eat a box of cookies.

6) **You feel enraged all day long but don't know why. What do you do to justify your feelings?**
   a) Blame it on hormones and try to relax.
   b) Blame everyone around you and spend the day shouting.
   c) Blame yourself and sit in your room all day.

See page 50 to find out what your reactions say about how you deal with anger!

Getting to the Source

Before people can deal with their anger, they need to get to its source. Only when a person knows the real triggers, or causes, of his or her anger can he or she develop strategies to deal with it.

KNOW YOUR TRIGGERS

One of the keys to handling anger is to know what tends to make you angry and when. This kind of self-awareness is something young children cannot do, and that is why they have temper tantrums. The peak age for angry feelings is three to four years old, but children this young do not know why they feel bad. They just let out the emotion.

TIP

If you know that something regularly annoys you, then find a solution. For example, if a sibling likes to talk through your favorite television show, talk to him or her about it calmly before the show starts, or record and watch the show while he or she is out.

Hidden feelings

It can be difficult to identify triggers, as often the thing that seems to have caused the anger may have just been the last straw, not the true trigger. For example, when asked to really think about an argument a girl had with a friend at school, she realized that the real reason she was upset was because everyone was watching. The other girl said the real reason she was angry was because she felt the argument meant that the first girl was not really her friend. In these cases the hidden causes beneath the anger were shame and loneliness. Putting emotions into words helps people figure out what it is they are really angry about.

If a bully knows what triggers a person's anger, the bully will keep using those weapons. Knowing these things are a trigger and deciding to react in a different way, like ignoring the bully, can be one way for the victim to deal with the situation.

Getting it
Right

Write down when, why, and where you feel anger building up.
For example, siblings may always annoy you when you are trying
to do your homework, or parents may nag you at bedtime when
you are tired. Each time you write something down, rate the
anger on a scale of 1 to 10 (with 10 being the angriest). Try to be
completely honest about what caused the anger and write down
if there were any background problems that may have been the
root cause of your anger.

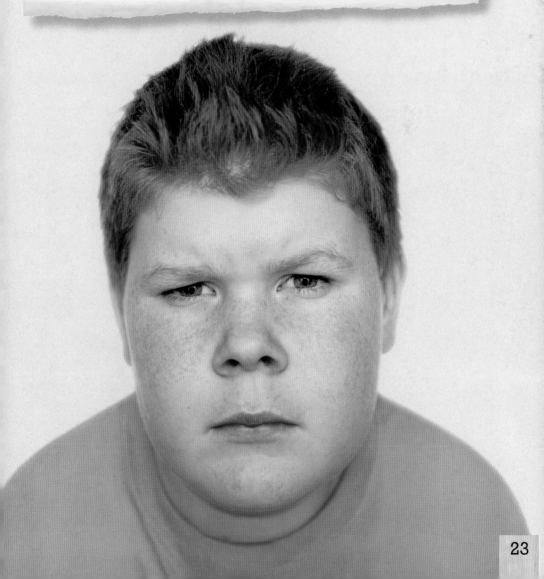

"I used to have a short fuse. I'm tall for my age. I used to push people around a little. I think people used to provoke me because I was big. After I nearly got banned from the football team after a fight, I decided to make a change. Now I take a deep breath and try to see things as they really are, rather than flying off the handle right away. I realize now that most people are just goofing around and that there is no need to be so defensive."

Zac, 15

Read the signs

There are usually specific warning signs when anger is building to a potentially uncontrollable level. Some people start to raise their voice, feel their heart pounding loudly in their chest, or breathe more quickly. Being aware of these signs can help you respond early and take better control of your anger. Reading and responding to the signs can save you pain and regret later if an argument gets out of control and you say or do things that you can never take back.

Interpret the situation

Besides looking to body signals to intercept anger, also take a cold, hard look at the situation. Are you **interpreting** the situation correctly? Is there another, equally believable interpretation of the situation? Is your reaction justified, and is it in proportion? For example, say someone bangs into you at a dance or throws something that hits you in the head. You are in pain and you fly into a rage, assuming that they did it on purpose and that they and their friends are laughing at you.

Getting it Right

When you know the warning signs that tell you you are getting angry, you can take some steps to calm down. If you know that feeling hot and flushed is a sign that anger is mounting, open a window to help cool you down. If you find you clench your fists and grit your teeth when anger is building, think about how these things increase your tension. If you can relax your hands and your mouth, you may end up feeling a little more relaxed, too.

Taking a moment to assess the situation gives people the chance to see a situation for what it really is and remain cool and calm.

People bump into each other in busy streets all the time. A few take it personally and get mad, but more people accept it as a normal hazard of city life!

TAKE RESPONSIBILITY

When people's anger gets out of control, they usually blame the person or event that made them angry, but no one really makes people angry. People are each responsible for the anger they feel. Taking responsibility means accepting that you create or maintain the situation itself that triggers your anger. Taking responsibility for your anger is a step toward dealing with it.

Rights and wrongs

Think about what you have a right to be angry about and what you do not. For example, some teenagers grow up in areas where crime and violence are common. They feel angry about the state of their neighborhood and the fact that they do not feel safe to go out. This is something that people have every right to feel angry about.

On the other hand, when a friend decides she no longer wants to go out to a party that you had planned to go to together, you have a right to feel disappointed and let down, and you can express those feelings, but you do not really have the right to be angry with that person. Everyone has the right to change his or her mind, and you should respect that—and remember that if you respect other people's choices, they will respect yours when you change your mind.

Know your rights!

Sometimes people get angry because they are unsure of what they have a right to feel or do. You have a right to:

- express (politely) your feelings and state your needs.

- be treated with respect.

- make mistakes. (But that also goes for other people—they have a right to make mistakes, too!)

- say "yes" or "no" for yourself.

- say when you do not understand something or when you disagree with someone.

If a teacher scolds you for something you did not do, act responsibly and sensibly. After class, politely ask to talk to the teacher and tell him or her that you were not talking and you would prefer not to have your record reflect something you did not do.

Taking responsibility for your feelings helps you deal with conflicts better. One way to take responsibility and help diffuse anger in others is to start sentences with "I" instead of "you." For example, don't say: "You make me angry because you put me down in front of our friends." Instead, say: "I get angry when I feel put down by your comments in front of our friends." Statements beginning with "I" show that you take responsibility for your feelings and that you are not simply dishing out blame.

Keeping Your Cool

This chapter explores some of the tactics you can use to manage your anger when faced with a trigger. Each person is unique, so you will need to try out some different options before you find the strategies that best work for you.

HOW TO COOL DOWN

Find ways to relax on a day-to-day basis. Listen to music that you like or that calms you, whether it is using headphones, stretching out on your bed and turning on the radio, or playing an instrument. Read a book or write a journal. Learn **yoga** or another non-strenuous exercise that relaxes your muscles and your mind and makes you feel calmer. Doing something relaxing every day helps you unwind and releases tension.

DID YOU KNOW?

There is a well-known saying that "laughter is the best medicine," and sometimes it can cure anger, too. If you can think about how silly a situation is, you might be able to see the humor in the situation and laugh instead of feeling enraged.

Have some fun

Sometimes life can feel a bit like a drag, especially when you are under pressure with exams or sports competitions. So, make sure you have some fun and laughter. Treat yourself kindly and give yourself weekly rewards, such as shopping, going to the movies, watching a sporting event, or having lunch with friends.

Having fun does not have to cost much—you can rent your favorite movies and invite a friend over for a comedy night, or get a group of pals together for a walk and a picnic. The idea is to make time every week to do something that makes you feel happy. Doing fun things regularly helps to keep you calm when you run into a situation that makes you angry.

A relaxation technique

1. Sit or lie down somewhere comfortable. Start to breathe slowly and deeply (see page 10).

2. First, tense (or tighten) and then relax the different parts of your body, starting with your feet and working upward. Tense and then relax the big toe of your right foot, then the second toe, third toe, fourth toe, fifth toe, bottom of your right foot, top of your right foot, and right heel. Take a deep breath in and, as you breathe out, relax your whole right foot. Then do this for your left foot and both your legs, followed by your fingers, hands, and arms. Finally, tense and relax your shoulders, then your neck, and finish off with your head. Constantly concentrate on feeling all of your muscles relax and loosen.

3. Replace distracting thoughts with an image of somewhere you have really enjoyed being, such as an empty beach.

4. Stay like this for as long as you wish, then take some deep breaths and open your eyes. Give yourself a few moments and get up slowly.

Finding ways to relax helps you get a good night's sleep, which also helps you to stay calm and cool in difficult situations.

TAKING CARE OF YOURSELF

This might sound obvious or too simple to be true, but eating properly, getting a good night's sleep, and getting exercise can all help you stay cool and calm.

Healthy eating

When we feel stressed, it is easy to reach for fast food or unhealthy snacks, but these only give us a short burst of energy and can contribute to feelings of stress. Eating healthy foods will keep your body and mind in balance.

"I took up boxing. When something makes me mad I take it out on the punching bag. I also go jogging, and the fresh air clears my head. I feel fitter and better about myself, too, so when people try to bring me down, I'm less likely to be bothered."

Matt, 13

Getting it Right

A healthy diet consists of carbohydrates at every meal, found in pastas and cereals, some proteins such as cheese and meat, a little fat, and plenty of vegetables and fruits to make your quota of vitamins and minerals.

Work it out!

Exercise helps relieve tension because it releases energy in a positive way. You could simply take a half-hour walk every day or take up a new sport. If you are tense it may be best to try a non-contact competitive sport, such as swimming or running.

DID YOU KNOW?

When you exercise it stimulates the release of chemicals in the brain called **endorphins**. Endorphins help the body control stress and put people in a good mood.

Being positive

Having a healthy outlook is just as important as being physically healthy. Try to be positive about yourself and don't give in to negative thoughts. Take pride in what you can do well and allow yourself to make mistakes.

For example, when working on your anger management, if you do lose your temper, don't be overcome with remorse. Cut yourself some slack and tell yourself that you will do better next time.

Remind yourself of the things you have done and do well and ask others for some positive reinforcement, too. Having good self-esteem gives you confidence and the belief that you can deal with difficult situations of any kind when they arise.

Some people find that hitting a punching bag is a good way to release anger.

Why sleep matters

Being angry or stressed takes energy and makes people feel exhausted. When people are tired they are more likely to lose their temper. A good night's sleep can give people the energy they need to cope with anger triggers when they occur. Teenagers often change their sleep patterns, preferring to stay up late and sleep later in the morning. However, on school nights or before a big game, it is important to get all the sleep you need.

Tackle Your Triggers

When you know which situations trigger, or cause, your anger, you can take steps to avoid them. Tackling your triggers in this way means there will be fewer times when you find yourself in a frustrating or annoying situation, and therefore fewer times when you let your anger get out of control.

TIME IT RIGHT

Sometimes you can avoid triggers simply by doing things on a different schedule. For example, if you and your parents always end up arguing when you discuss problems last thing at night, try to change the time when you talk to them. Explain that it is not that you will not talk about that issue, but that you are tired or distracted and would prefer to discuss it over breakfast. Or if you are really not a morning person and always end up in a shouting match because you are late, set your alarm for five minutes earlier and make yourself get up to avoid the last-minute arguments.

Avoidance tactics

Avoiding situations that make you mad is another way to tackle your triggers. For example, if a friend always seems to ignore you when she is with another mutual friend, avoid seeing them together. Or if someone gets angry because his younger sister always hangs around when he has friends over, perhaps he could arrange to see his friends somewhere else or get his parents to take his sister to a friend's house when he has his friends over.

Alternative choices

Finding alternative ways of doing things is another way to avoid your anger triggers. For example, if you always start the day angry because a friend is always late to pick you up, catch a bus instead or find another ride. Or if you have a long bus journey to school that annoys you, read a book or play music on headphones and tune out for the trip.

Try to avoid situations that always make you angry. If you sense your sister is in the mood for making you angry, stay out of her way.

If your anger trigger happens to be a buildup of stress, aim to solve little problems as they come along instead of allowing them to develop into big ones. For example, rather than avoiding large parts of a project until you are late and teachers and parents are nagging you and making you angry, try to do small bits of work more often to get on top of it. That way you will be in control and the stress will not build up.

HAVE A PLAN

It really helps to have a plan or technique that you can use to calm yourself when something happens that suddenly makes you angry. Flashpoints that occur suddenly and unexpectedly can be especially difficult to cope with because they catch you off-guard.

For example, say you are enjoying yourself and feeling relaxed, and suddenly someone who has a grudge against you joins the party and starts trying to pick a fight. What do you do?

The best way to be prepared for flashpoints like this is to have a plan of action that you always try to follow.

Take a deep breath and, in that moment, think whether your interpretation of the situation is correct, or if there is another equally valid interpretation. Remind yourself that you have a choice about how to react. You can choose whether to be angry and let that person spoil your evening, or you can choose another route. Think—if your best friend were in this situation, what advice would you give him or her?

When faced with a flashpoint situation, like being fouled during a soccer match, stop and think. If you go with your initial reaction and hit back, you might be ejected.

Flashpoint focus

If you find yourself in a situation in which you realize that you will not be able to control your rising anger to take stock of the situation, walk away. Simply tell the other person that you are too angry to talk to him or her right now and get out of there. If you cannot leave the room, close your eyes or turn away, count to 10, and breathe deeply. Just give yourself a bit of space to take back control. If the urge to lash out at something is overwhelming, release that anger by hitting a cushion or shouting and screaming, ideally somewhere where you are alone and others cannot see or hear you.

Getting it Right

Experiment with alternative ways of reacting to situations that make you angry. One way to do this is to first watch how other people react to situations. Think of someone who handles disappointment or frustration more constructively than you do and use that person as a role model. Think about how he or she behaves and practice doing the same yourself.

TIP

Some people find that it helps to learn a **mantra** that you can say to yourself in your head to get yourself thinking positively. It might sound a little weird, but it really can help. Try saying one of the following to yourself, over and over, when you feel angry:

- "I can handle this. If I start getting upset I know what to do."

- "I don't need to prove myself, relax."

- "I have a right to be angry, but I can control my anger."

- "He's trying to get me angry in order to make me look bad. I'm not going to give him that satisfaction."

express yourself

If you feel angry about something, you have every right to express that anger. The key to expressing yourself well is to be **assertive** and not aggressive. Being assertive means saying what you think, want, and feel in a direct and honest way, without intentionally hurting anyone's feelings.

Being assertive

When people are angry they often go on the attack and shout insults. To be assertive, speak calmly, clearly, and say how you feel. Say directly why you don't like something. Instead of saying the first angry thing that comes into your head, be specific. For example: "I am angry with you because when you told that person that I like him I felt embarrassed." It also helps to look people in the eye. Concentrate on breathing normally and speaking at a regular conversational volume. Do not raise your voice, as this can turn a civil conversation into a full-blown argument.

"A lot of things still make me angry, but I deal with it better. When I'm angry I write. I say all the nasty, mean things I'm feeling on a big piece of paper and then I rip it up. Try it—it feels surprisingly good!"

Chris, 14

Getting it Right

- Express your opinions and feelings.

- Say "no" without feeling guilty. It is okay to disagree with people, even friends.

- Ask for what you want clearly but firmly.

- Keep what you want to say clear and to the point. Avoid long explanations.

- There is no need to apologize if you feel you are in the right.

- Be polite but firm.

Being creative

Another healthy way to express anger is creatively, perhaps through art or writing. Some people find that it helps to let their feelings out by writing about them in a journal, or by creating poetry or lyrics. Some people write letters about their anger. Let all your feelings pour out into a letter, but don't send it. Read it again the next day. You may want to rip it up to rid yourself of those toxic emotions. If you still feel strongly about the issue, edit the letter so it sounds calm and assertive, and then send it.

Many people draw, paint, or do other creative projects as an outlet for their anger.

Getting it
Wrong

Swearing, screaming, and shouting in anger elevates situations and the people in them into a greater and greater frenzy of rage. This kind of aggressive release actually fans the flames of anger instead of solving the problem. Pretty soon the aggression takes over, and the cause of the anger is lost in a verbal cloud of abuse.

Meet and Talk It Out

When anger is caused by an argument or conflict with another person or group, it can help to set up a meeting with that person or group so you can talk it through. The idea of a meeting like this is to find a solution to the problem, so it is very important to be prepared so that you can keep a lid on your anger and get your views heard.

Before the meeting

Choose the time and place of a meeting carefully. Find somewhere peaceful, where you will not be disturbed and where it feels relaxed. Before you go, think about what exactly it is you are angry about and what you want to achieve, but be realistic. You cannot expect the other person or group to do exactly what you want or take all the blame. Expect and allow the other person or people to say how they feel, too—all involved need to respect each other's right to have their own different feelings about an issue.

During the meeting

During the meeting keep your body language assertive, not aggressive. Do not clench your fists, look away, or sit back with your arms crossed as if you are not listening. Breathe deeply to keep calm and listen to the other person. This may mean you have to accept some criticism, which can be hard. However, the more carefully you listen to others, the less likely you are to misinterpret their statements. Listening to other people will make them more likely to listen to you and accept your criticisms.

After the meeting

If the meeting did not go well and you did not reach a **resolution**, you can arrange another meeting and perhaps ask for a **mediator** to join you. Whether or not the meeting solved the problem, make sure you reward yourself afterward for handling the situation so well and managing your anger assertively—for example, with a treat like a trip to the movies.

Getting it Right

A mediator helps people or groups reach a solution to an issue they are arguing about. A mediator is someone who is neutral and who does not take sides. A mediator listens to both sides of the argument and encourages the people in the dispute to speak calmly and stay focused on the facts, rather than shouting angry words at each other. Some schools have mediators who step in to help classmates resolve conflicts, or you could ask a friend to be a mediator—as long as both sides agree to the choice.

To solve an ongoing problem of a sibling taking her stuff, Holly called a meeting with her brother and asked her aunt and uncle to sit in as mediators. She and her brother talked through the problem, and he agreed not to take her stuff again without asking.

Group therapy sessions often help people by showing them that others have had similar experiences to them. Relating to people in this way can reduce the sense of shame or guilt that people who have angry outbursts often feel. It can also help people to feel less alone.

SEEING A COUNSELOR

Counselors and **therapists** are trained to support people through complicated or bad times, such as a trauma like divorce or death. They also help people deal with bullying or depression and with compulsions such as overeating. Some people choose to go to a counselor to help them manage their anger before it gets out of control. You can find a counselor, therapist, or support group in the phone book, or ask your school or health center for a recommendation.

Getting it Right

Whatever course of action you decide to take to deal with your anger, use a support network. Tell the important people in your life what you are feeling and what you are doing so that they can support you and cut you some slack if you lapse into old negative patterns.

What is therapy?

When people see a counselor about their anger problems, the counselor mostly listens to them. All of the conversations they have are private and confidential. After several visits, when trust has built up, many people find it a relief to be able to talk to someone, outside their usual circle of family and friends, with complete honesty. Together, the counselor and the client figure out a range of methods and tactics that the individual can use to help cope with trigger situations.

Group therapy

Instead of seeing a counselor on a one-on-one basis, some people choose to go to group therapy. This is when you work with a group of people who have similar problems. It can help to talk problems through with people who understand what you are going through. It also helps to know that you are not the only one who has trouble controlling anger.

HOW DO YOU COPE?

1) Someone starts to tease you about a sore point. You are really not in the mood. How do you deal with it?
   a) Shout insults back.
   b) Send them an anonymous, nasty text message later.
   c) Tell them you are not interested in their comments and leave the room.

2) Your mom forgets to record the final episode of your favorite television show. What do you do?
   a) Lose your temper and shout at her.
   b) Say nothing, but sulk about it for hours.
   c) Ask around your friends to see if any of them recorded it.

3) Your brother borrows and scratches one of your favorite CDs. What do you do?
   a) Break something of his.
   b) Refuse to speak to him for a week.
   c) Ask him to buy a replacement.

See page 50 to find out how well you cope in frustrating situations.

Other People's Anger

Sometimes it is not your own anger that you have to deal with, but other people's. It can be very difficult when parents or other people close to you take out their problems on you or on other members of your family.

LIVING WITH PARENTAL ANGER

Like everyone else, parents can get angry. Sometimes this anger gets out of control, perhaps because of an event like losing a job, the death of a friend, or simply because they are just not getting along with one another. Some parents' anger is explosive and out of proportion to what sets them off, especially if fueled by alcohol or drugs. A parent's anger may be aimed at a child or partner. Sometimes it is in the form of verbal abuse, such as constant criticism, which can make other family members feel like failures. Some parents release their anger in the form of physical abuse, such as slapping or hitting.

Angry role models

Sometimes having angry parents is the reason that teenagers have a tough time dealing with anger themselves. Other parents bottle up their anger and expect their children to do so, too. Children learn to behave in a similar way to their parents. They may see their parents argue and abuse each other in anger, and so they grow up thinking that name-calling, screaming, or hitting is normal if you are angry. They may even grow up thinking that threatening and bullying someone is an acceptable means of getting your own way.

Getting it Wrong

Physical abuse is against the law. Hitting people never makes problems go away, and if one of your parents uses violence against you or anyone else, there is a risk someone could get seriously hurt, and so it has to stop. You need to talk to a trusted family member, such as a favorite aunt, a teacher, or a close family friend about your concerns and get help.

Getting it Right

- Stop the cycle. Just because they are shouting at you, this does not mean you have to shout or throw insults back.

- Wait until they have calmed down and then calmly and clearly explain how their anger is affecting the family. Try using "I" or "me," such as, "I can tell you're angry" or, "You being angry makes me feel frightened and upset."

- Discuss constructive ways they can deal with their anger, like taking time to go for a walk or changing how they do things.

- If you are really concerned, when things are calm and quiet, bring up the idea of individual or **family therapy**.

Some parents manage to keep calm with their children, but fight with each other. When parents express anger aggressively and violently toward each other, they still hurt their children emotionally.

Friends and siblings

Friends, brothers and sisters, or even complete strangers might get angry with you for many reasons. Here we look at some ways to deal with other people's anger.

However hard you try to avoid them, you will inevitably come across situations in which, even though you try to stay calm and resolve a problem with someone, all the person wants to do is shout and fight.

It may be that the person who is angry has a fair point. Perhaps there is something you can do differently next time and you can learn from that person's anger. Or maybe that person just needs your extra support because he or she is upset.

Imagine you get an angry phone call from a friend after not seeing or calling him or her for a while. Instead of shouting back, you could understand why the friend is hurt and choose to apologize instead.

Tough love

Sometimes it is easier to agree with your friends rather than contradict them, even if you disagree with them. You may do this because you do not want to upset them, or because you fear they will not be friends with you anymore if you criticize them.

It is hard to be tough, but always discourage destructive behavior. For example, if a friend is angry with someone and starts to talk about ways to get back at him or her, you need to make it clear that you think your friend would be wiser to deal with the problem directly or let it go. Let your friend know how you feel, but in a cool and calm way.

TIP

If you think a friend is in danger of doing something really stupid that might get him or her into serious trouble, and he or she won't listen to you, then you really need to tell someone else or get someone else to talk to your friend, too.

If a friend is angry with you, try to see his or her point of view and perhaps apologize. Later, when everyone has calmed down, you can explain if you did not like the way the situation was handled.

Getting it **Wrong**

Adding fuel to the fire of someone's anger is likely to make that person more angry. Most people can read the signs that tell us when it is best to back off and let a person cool down. Avoid doing or saying things that you know will make someone mad. Upsetting someone deliberately is a bad idea, as you risk sparking an angry outburst.

Summing It Up

Anger is a powerful emotion, but is a part of life that everyone needs to learn to deal with effectively. There is not a "one-size-fits-all" solution, and each individual needs to figure out what is the right solution for him or her. If you have problems controlling your rage, remember that you are not alone—many people, including celebrities, have to work at controlling their anger.

In The News

Celebrities are often in the news for losing their temper with reporters, photographers, and others. Some, such as the actor Russell Crowe, have even been arrested for assault when they have let their anger get out of control.

In 2006 British supermodel Naomi Campbell did five days of community service for throwing a jewel-encrusted cell phone at her maid's head. After two days of anger management classes, Campbell said, "I feel sorry and I am really going to learn from my mistakes." However, in 2008 she received another community service sentence after lashing out when an airline lost her luggage!

Victims of anger

Sometimes people with anger issues find that it helps to put themselves in their victims' shoes, to meet and talk to them to find out what it is like to be on the receiving end of anger.

Victims of anger often feel like victims of bullying. Even if they have done something wrong, they do not deserve to be insulted or treated badly. Everyone makes mistakes.

Victims of anger are usually not the cause of anger anyway, but are often in the wrong place at the wrong time.

"Anger doesn't lead anywhere. You have to be in a position to be able to bring your temperament and adrenaline under control."

Russell Crowe, actor

Controlling your temper means you can avoid getting a bad reputation for anger. Naomi Campbell has become almost as famous for her short-fused temper as she is for being a fashion supermodel.

LIVE AND LEARN

Learning to control anger takes time, and the best way to learn is from individual experience. As you test out new ways of dealing with your anger, you will find out what works.

Ask yourself if you are reacting differently to triggers now.

- Are you less angry than you used to be?

- Do you feel better about yourself?

If the answers to these questions are "yes," then think about what you have been doing differently and keep using those techniques.

If things are not working out, don't give up or be hard on yourself. You simply have not found the right system yet and just need to keep experimenting.

Time and trust

In addition to giving yourself time, you need to use your support network— your friends and family—to help you gain control over your anger. Angry people are sometimes defensive and feel as though other people are out to annoy or criticize them. Try to trust that the people who care about you have your best interests at heart, even if they sometimes say the wrong things. If they know what you are trying to achieve, they will give you their support, and that can really help.

Getting it Right

"Sorry" is said to be the hardest word, but once you get the hang of using it, it is also the easiest way out of trouble! Controlling your temper is hard, and we all have slip-ups, but if you can take responsibility for how you acted—and apologize— most people will be quick to forgive and forget. But say it like you really mean it!

"My positive way of dealing with my anger is to talk about it. If I can't talk to the person who made me angry, I talk to a friend or anyone who'll listen! Getting it off my chest helps me, and hearing other people's opinions really gets things in perspective."

Jasmine, 13

Being angry can make you miss out on some good times. It may sound like a tired cliché, but we should make the most of every day.

ARE YOU TAKING CONTROL?

1) **One of your anger triggers is listening to people talking on the bus. How do you manage this?**
   a) Wear headphones or listen to music when you take the bus.
   b) Glare at people talking on the bus and tell them to shut up.
   c) Walk instead of taking the bus.

2) **A friend of yours is in danger of harming himself or someone else because of his anger. What do you do?**
   a) Talk to a trusted teacher or family member about the situation.
   b) Decide to help him with his plans.
   c) Ignore him.

3) **Your mom loses her temper and shouts at you because your room is messy. You are running late and need to leave for school. How do you deal with the situation?**
   a) Ask if you can clean your room after school and tell your mom later that you didn't like it when she shouted.
   b) Shout back and insult your mom.
   c) Leave the house and get to school on time.

4) **You feel as though you are still unable to control your anger. What actions do you take to change?**
   a) Ask your doctor or school to put you in contact with a counselor or therapist.
   b) Spend the afternoon punching pillows.
   c) Ignore your feelings.

See page 50 to find out how well you are managing to take control of your anger.

Results

IS YOUR ANGER A PROBLEM?
For page 7

- **If you answered "yes" to any or all of these questions:** your anger may be a problem. The first step in managing your anger is admitting that it is an issue.

- **If you answered "no" to all of these questions:** you seem to have your anger under control.

HOW WELL DO YOU REACT?
For page 21

- **If you answered mostly a),** you keep your cool! You, like everyone, get angry, but you also manage that anger well.

- **If you answered mostly b),** you need to chill out! You tend to express anger in a negative, often aggressive way.

- **If you answered mostly c),** you bottle it up! Think about discussing what makes you angry with someone else before it starts to eat you up.

HOW DO YOU COPE?
For page 41

- **If you answered mostly a),** you are still letting your anger take over. Try to come up with an action plan so you can start behaving less aggressively.

- **If you answered mostly b),** you are holding your anger in. Think of ways you can release your anger by discussing the things that make you angry with others.

- **If you answered mostly c),** you are well on the road to dealing with your anger constructively.

ARE YOU TAKING CONTROL?
For page 49

- **If you answered mostly a),** you are gaining the upper hand on your anger and act sensibly when faced with anger-fueled situations. Continue to find ways to keep cool and calm.

- **If you answered mostly b),** you haven't found the right system to best deal with your anger and you just need to keep experimenting.

- **If you answered mostly c),** you are getting there, but tend to bottle up your anger instead of dealing with it properly and don't always act sensibly in anger-fueled situations.

20 Things to Remember

1 Know what annoys you. Know where, when, and how it annoys you so that you can avoid anger triggers.

2 If you are feeling angry, talk about how you are feeling with a friend, parent, or teacher.

3 Be positive about yourself and focus on your good points.

4 Use self-control. Don't let yourself give in to knee-jerk reactions. Think before you act.

5 Think about your body's reactions to anger. Take long, deep breaths and unclench those fists. Relaxing your body will help relax your reactions.

6 Try writing your feelings down. Read them through before confronting others.

7 Take care of yourself by exercising and eating well.

8 Make time for quality rest and relaxation. Being tired is enough to make anyone grumpy.

9 When you feel angry, take a moment to consider your options and think carefully about what the outcomes of any actions will be.

10 Express yourself well: talk clearly and calmly, and do not raise your voice.

11 Confront the problem, not the person—think and talk about the problem, don't attack the person.

12 Learn to compromise. If you are prepared to give a little, people are much more likely to meet you halfway.

13 Accept that you, too, may have to take some criticisms when you argue.

14 Know that the real point of telling someone what makes you angry is to find a solution to a problem, not just to let off steam.

15 Use empathy. Put yourself in another person's shoes. Seeing things from his or her point of view can help you to accept compromises.

16 Learn from the ways other people deal with potentially explosive situations. Watch friends or classmates deal with things that make them angry. What tactics do they use?

17 When there is a serious problem with someone or something, call a meeting to talk it out. Plan what to say and how to explain the reasons for your anger.

18 Act assertively, not aggressively. It is okay to be firm, to keep arguing your side if you are sure you are right, as long as you do not let your anger take over.

19 Use a support network when trying to take control of your anger. Ask friends and family for help. Perhaps they could gently touch you on the shoulder when they see you getting out of control—just to remind you to stay in charge of your emotions.

20 Learn to say you are sorry and mean it. "Sorry" is a small word that can get big results.

Further Information

www.mayoclinic.com/health/anger-management/MH00102
Get advice about understanding and managing your anger.

www.youngwomenshealth.org/anger.html
Girls can get advice about anger management and health issues here.

www.mentalhelp.net/poc/center_index.php?id=116&cn=116
This site offers comprehensive information about anger—how it works and how to control it.

http://wso.williams.edu/~atimofey/self_mutilation/
Find out about self-mutilation—its causes as well as treatment options.

http://kidshealth.org/kid/grow/body_stuff/puberty.html
This website explores issues you face when going through puberty.

BOOKS/GUIDES

Bickerstaff, Linda. *Stress: Coping in a Changing World.* New York: Rosen, 2007.

Crist, James. *Mad: How to Deal with Your Anger and Get Respect.* Minneapolis: Free Spirit, 2008.

Diconsiglio, John. *Out of Control: How to Handle Anger—Yours and Everyone Else's.* New York: Franklin Watts, 2007.

Esherick, Joan. *Balancing Act: A Teen's Guide to Managing Stress.* Philadelphia: Mason Crest, 2005.

Hipp, Earl. *Fighting Invisible Tigers: A Stress Management Guide for Teens.* Minneapolis: Free Spirit, 2008.

Simmonds, Jennifer. *Seeing Red: An Anger Management and Peacemaking Curriculum for Kids.* Gabriola, BC: New Society, 2003.

Wilde, Jerry. *Hot Stuff to Help Kids Chill Out: The Anger Management Book.* Richmond, IN: LGR, 1997.

Glossary

abuse mistreatment of another person, animal, or thing, either physically or emotionally

adrenaline hormone released into the body in certain situations, usually when a person is physically or emotionally distressed or angry

allergy condition in which the body has an exaggerated response to a substance such as dust, a particular food, or medicine

assertive saying what you want clearly and confidently

compromise come to a decision midway between two extremes

compulsion urge to behave in a way that you know you shouldn't

counselor person who gives guidance and advice

depression condition in which someone has continual, prolonged feelings of sadness, despair, loss of energy, and difficulty dealing with normal daily life

endorphin substance released by the brain that gives a sense of happiness and well-being

family therapy therapy that treats an entire family and aims to improve the way they relate to and communicate with one another

flashpoint point at which someone's fury might be triggered

hormone substance produced by the body that acts as a chemical messenger relaying instructions to body organs to tell them to stop or start certain processes

interpreting way of understanding something that is not immediately obvious

mantra sound or phrase chanted during meditation

mediator person who tries to help two sides in conflict come to a decision or find a solution that is acceptable to both of them

motivation push that gives someone the desire to achieve a goal or join in an activity

pre-menstrual syndrome condition that can happen around the time of a woman's period, when she might feel tired, get mood swings, and feel angry or depressed

puberty time of life when a child gradually changes into an adult, which can start any time between the ages of 10 and 18

resolution finding a solution to a problem

self-esteem feeling of self-worth, self-confidence, and self-respect

stress physical, mental, or emotional strain or tension

suppress hold emotions in and not show them—to "bottle things up"

therapist professional who gives advice about emotional problems

trigger cause a reaction

vandalism destruction or damage to someone else's property

yoga form of exercise and relaxation that includes movement, controlled breathing, and mental training

Index